COACH YOURSELF BETTER, FAST

PRESENT LIKE A PRO

Based on *Executive Presentations*
by Jacqui Harper

First published in Great Britain by Practical Inspiration Publishing, 2024

© Jacqui Harper and Practical Inspiration Publishing, 2024

The moral rights of the author have been asserted

ISBN   9781788606769   (print)
            9781788606783   (epub)
            9781788606776   (Kindle)

All rights reserved. This book, or any portion thereof, may not be reproduced without the express written permission of the publisher.

Every effort has been made to trace copyright holders and to obtain their permission for the use of copyright material. The publisher apologizes for any errors or omissions and would be grateful if notified of any corrections that should be incorporated in future reprints or editions of this book.

Want to bulk-buy copies of this book for your team and colleagues? We can customize the content and co-brand *Present Like a Pro* to suit your business's needs.

Please email info@practicalinspiration.com for more details.

Practical Inspiration Publishing

Contents

Series introduction v

Introduction 1

Day 1: Begin powerfully 4

Day 2: Reinforce ideas 21

Day 3: Involve the audience
       (and manage your script!) 30

Day 4: Be bold 46

Day 5: End powerfully 54

Day 6: Vocal presence 60

Day 7: Body language and style 77

Day 8: Gratitude 99

Day 9: Self-coaching 107

Day 10: Nerve management, and solutions 124

Conclusion: My top ten tips 135

Endnotes 139

Series introduction

Welcome to *6-Minute Smarts*!

This is a series of very short books with one simple purpose: to introduce you to ideas that can make life and work better, and to give you time and space to think about how those ideas might apply to your life and work.

Each book introduces you to ten powerful ideas, but ideas on their own are useless – that's why each idea is followed by self-coaching questions to help you work out the 'so what?' for you in just six minutes of exploratory writing. What's exploratory writing? It's the kind of writing you do just for yourself, fast and free, without worrying what anyone else thinks. It's not just about getting ideas out of your head and onto paper where you can see them, it's about finding new connections and insights as you write. This is where the magic happens.

Find out more...

Introduction

This book provides a powerful development tool for one of the most significant areas of competence for leaders: executive presence.

- You might be an experienced and successful leader who wants to develop the specific area of presenting.
- You might be a newly promoted executive going into general management with new challenges and expectations.
- You might speak to international audiences.
- You might present at board meetings.
- You might be seeking new ideas for your presentations.
- You might be an emerging leader eager to support ambitions with stronger presentation skills.

- You might be an executive coach supporting clients with issues relating to their executive presence.
- You might be on an exciting learning journey on an MBA programme or other business course, in which case this book will support you alongside your studies and ahead of your next role.

Whether you're an experienced leader who wants to develop a specific area of presenting, or an emerging leader seeking new ideas for presentations, welcome! I've written this book for anyone seeking inspiration and guidance in effective executive presentations.

What exactly do I mean when I say 'presentation'?

Just for the sake of being crystal clear, executive presentations come in all shapes and sizes, whether it's the set-piece conference talk to several hundred people or intimate meetings with fewer than a hundred participants. Online presentations are very much in the mix, whether audio or video. Formal or informal board meetings are clearly places where

Introduction

executives are presenting ideas. Indeed, you can present information to just a few colleagues.

You're ready to start. Over the next ten chapters (ten days, if you fancy treating this as a mini-course) you're going to discover ten key principles of executive presentations and experiment with using them for yourself.

Let's go!

Day 1
Begin powerfully

Begin a presentation powerfully and you have a huge advantage. A weak start, on the other hand, can be very hard to turn around. Let's look at that advantage with effective ways to connect quickly and deeply to an audience.

BRIBE model

I've created an easy-to-remember tool called BRIBE to help you communicate clear and compelling ideas. We'll follow each of these five ideas in the first five days.

B = Begin Powerfully
R = Reinforce Ideas
I = Involve the Audience

Begin powerfully

B = Be Bold
E = End Powerfully

This chapter shows four ways to make the strongest start to an executive presentation:

- The emotional objective
- The information objective
- The preview
- The hook

The emotional objective

> 'I've learned that people will forget what you said, people will forget what you did, but people will never forget how you made them feel.'
>
> Maya Angelou[1]

Executive speakers would do well to follow the wise words of writer Maya Angelou. Instead, too often people start preparing a presentation by focusing on the objective – the point or ideas they want the audience to take away.

Start with the emotional objective. Think about what you want the audience to *feel* when you've finished speaking; for example, excited, uncomfortable, reassured or reflective. Consider ways to evoke those emotions. At your disposal are the words you choose, your storytelling technique, the structure of the presentation, the themes, the slide deck, your voice, body language, facial expressions and your appearance. All these points are discussed throughout this book.

Working with an emotional objective can help create a deep connection with an audience. It establishes the kind of rapport that makes an audience more likely to want to listen to what you have to say.

This technique even goes back as far as the Greek philosopher Aristotle. In his book *The Art of Rhetoric* he identifies three tools for effective speech: argument, character and emotion.

The primary emotions are usually identified as happiness, sadness, fear, anger, surprise, disgust and trust. These feel a little limiting to me, though, so I turn to feelings, sometimes called compounds of emotions.[2]

I often show participants a chart listing human *feelings* and I encourage them to select the feeling(s) most relevant to the executive presentation they're creating. I remind them that there's one feeling relevant to all presentations: trust. See Figure 1 for others:

Begin powerfully

Glad	Hopeful	Able	Curious
Happy	Expectant	Confident	Good
Delighted	Relieved	Powerful	Great
Joyful	Satisfied	Interested	Compassion
Elated	Certain	Awe	Sympathy
Thrilled	Assured	Inspired	Empathy
Comfortable	Eager	Uncomfortable	Annoyed
Excited	Enthusiastic	Nervous	Shocked
Positive	Concerned	Thoughtful	Unhappy
Impressed	Challenged	Cheerful	Pride

Fig. 1: List of human feelings

Without doubt the most effective way of achieving emotional objectives in presentations is through storytelling, which releases oxytocin, making us more empathic and more cooperative.

Mapping emotions

You could use one overarching emotional objective for an entire presentation or you could map specific emotional objectives to different parts of the presentation. For example, you might want surprise at the beginning of a presentation, reassurance in the middle and excitement as the emotional objective at the end.

Figure 2 shows an emotional map of a lecture I give on executive presence:

Element of presentation	Emotional objective	Ways to generate the emotions
Beginning	Trust	Tell them a short story of my lifelong love affair with communication – to understand my expertise and passion for the subject.
Beginning	Enthusiasm	Smile and speak with vocal energy, facial animation and gestures.
Middle	Thoughtful	Give the audience new ways to think about the structure of a presentation by sharing the BRIBE model.
Middle	Thoughtful	Ask questions – both real and rhetorical.
Middle	Surprise	Use unexpected examples to illustrate ideas. For example, I sometimes show a short video of international rapper Kanye West accepting a music award, because it's an exceptional example of how to end a speech.

Begin powerfully

End	Inspiration	Close with an inspiring quote such as an extract from the inaugural speech of the late Nelson Mandela. He in turn borrowed it from American writer and women's advocate Marianne Williamson. It talks beautifully about letting go of fear and owning your power and talent.

Fig. 2: Mapping emotional objectives

The information objective or WIIFM

Now let's look at the information objective using WIIFM (pronounced 'wiff-mm'). It simply stands for What's In It For Me. The 'me' in this instance is the audience, not the speaker. This is about putting yourself into the minds of an audience. What will the audience gain from your presentation and why is it so relevant to them?

Be explicit about the WIIFM and deliver it within three or so minutes of starting a presentation. Don't take too long making clear what's in it for the audience, otherwise you risk them disengaging. In the early moments of a presentation it's instinctive to wonder where a speaker is going; if that curiosity is satisfied in good time it's a promising start.

The WIIFM is more a global perspective of a presentation or the big picture. If the audience take one thing away from your presentation that clearly benefits them – what is it? A well-chosen WIIFM will give your audience a powerful reason to listen to you.

The preview

The preview gives clarity to ideas and keeps the audience engaged. Without clarity it can take a lot of work to rescue things if the audience doesn't know what you're talking about and why.

The preview effectively fills in the blanks that might be created by the objectives. The objectives are by their nature general, global points and it won't be long before an audience needs to know more. The preview gives the audience an understanding of how you've organized your thinking: the structure, the sequence, the approach.

An agenda slide does the job well and takes the form of a list with bullet points. This format is fine and is one to keep in the portfolio. The preview can, however, be delivered effectively without any slides

Begin powerfully

at all. I call this style of speaking 'naked', because it can feel like speaking without 'protection', but it will make you work hard at being crystal clear in your messaging. It enables you to deeply engage the audience at a crucial time in the speech; that is, when you're establishing connection. Slides can be distracting and interfere with the delicate relationship-building taking place.

If you're not quite ready for no slides, then making slides work better is a good option. Keeping words to a minimum will help. Having no more than four words per line helps the audience scan the slide quickly.

A picture-only preview can be effective, providing the image is clear, has impact and is totally relevant to the points you're making. Having an image-only preview means the audience is less distracted and, more than that, it means the audience *has* to listen more closely to understand what the picture means and where the presentation is going.

The hook

An effective hook will help the audience connect to the theme or subject of the presentation but devising one is often deeply frustrating and exhilarating. The frustration comes from the process of considering lots of different types of hooks and feeling that for one reason or another they don't quite work. The exhilaration happens when you find the hook that's just right for the presentation and the audience. Hooks may include quotes, powerful images, surprise, you, curiosity.

Quotes

Quotes can be words from a famous speaker or a business leader, or quotes from a poem or literature. Shakespeare is a popular choice in executive presentations because his plays are so well known and themes such as power, leadership, challenge, conflict, adversity and hope are ripe for visionary presentations. But think about more diverse and unexpected sources too.

There are many sites providing inspirational business quotes – you need never be short of the right quote for the right occasion.

Powerful images

A speaker from the British Foreign Office used a powerful image at the start of a presentation of a

Begin powerfully

protester about to be struck violently in the head by a soldier.

The image of the vicious strike was frozen in mid-action and drew gasps of horror from the audience. Our brains couldn't help taking us to the grim inevitability of what happened next. The image made us want to learn more about the reasons for the violence, so we were more than ready for the political analysis that followed.

Surprise

I recall a speaker whose purpose was to get staff to change wasteful practices in the workplace. The speaker scanned the room dramatically, paused and then set light to a real £5 note. This surprising start was a powerful way to connect the audience to the theme of wasting money.

Using surprise means that our brain gets to work straight away trying to figure out what's happening and what it means. It can be dramatic, subtle or anywhere in between.

A more subtle example is to take something familiar and add something surprising to it. Many people know the phrase 'I came, I saw, I conquered', attributed to the powerful Roman general, Julius

Caesar, and quoted by Rosalind in Shakespeare's *As You Like It*. The quote could be reused in a presentation with the words 'I came, I saw, I cried'. As we cry in pain or from happiness, the quote can be the start of a discussion about business performance that causes concern or brings joy. The trick is making sure the adapted version is clearly linked to the original.[3]

One of the most surprising hooks I've come across was at a travel industry presentation. The presentation was about Bali and the speaker's hook was the sense of smell. He had the aroma of neroli (orange blossom) wafting throughout the meeting room as he started speaking. I've never forgotten it.

You

You can use your presence to deliver a powerful beginning and it doesn't always need to be all bells and whistles to be effective.

I recently saw a speaker (Russ Hudson, a world expert on *The Enneagram*) who simply stood at the front of the conference room while participants took to their seats. He looked relaxed and smiling. There was something else about his presence I couldn't quite identify. My best guess was that he seemed 'peaceful'. There were no slide decks or handouts. As

Begin powerfully

he was about to start he *sat down* on a chair. What followed was one of the best business seminars I've ever attended: engaging, challenging, exciting, funny and richly informative. Somehow we knew we were in for a treat from the understated hook.

If you're seeking a high-impact, low-frills hook, let me introduce BLAB. It helps speakers get control at the beginning of their presentation when nerves are most likely to kick in. It forces you to slow down, breathe deeply to fuel the voice and engage eye contact.

BLAB

When I'm teaching this I get my participant to start 'off stage' (at the side of the room) and walk to the centre of the room. It's more effective if the pace of walking is measured, purposeful and energetic.

I insist there's no speaking while walking as I see too many instances of speakers diminishing their impact on entrance. When you arrive at the podium you pause and BLAB:

B – Breathe (take a full diaphragm breath)
L – Look into the audience and around the room
A – And pause
B – Begin speaking

What a deceptively simple technique! Indeed, BLAB is so fundamental to making an executive presentation start well that I'd argue that it's actually best practice for starting *any* presentation.

When you want a more dynamic hook, focus on presence. Pay attention to what the audience experience of you before you've said a single word. This means making use of body language, gestures, facial expressions, your energy level and your breathing.

Appearance

What you wear and your overall appearance can transform your impact. As always it's about detail: accessories, grooming, the quality, cut and styling of clothes. And colour. Colour is virtually the first thing an audience notices when you walk on stage. Colours can signal power, authority and confidence.

Curiosity

If you get the curiosity hook right it piques interest and is quick and efficient at connecting to the core message of a presentation. You can generate curiosity by asking a question, holding a prop or showing a slide with an unexplained statistic, fact or picture.

Begin powerfully

For example, when I deliver a course on presentations, the first slide I show my participants is a painting of a distinguished-looking guy in a flowing robe (from ancient history) and I ask the class to guess who he is and why he's so important to our training session. Some may guess his name correctly but very few know why he's relevant to business meetings; the important thing is that the energy rises while competitive participants make smart guesses about the mystery man.

Once we've identified that the man is in fact Aristotle, the Ancient Greek philosopher and scientist, it's easy to bring in his highly relevant ideas on the art of public speaking. He tells us that great presentations happen when three things are present:

- Pathos – an emotional connection between speaker and audience.
- Logos – a sequence of ideas that's well structured and well crafted.
- Ethos – a speaker with a positive and credible presence.

The very process of getting participants to guess means I'm engaging their minds and drawing them into the presentation.

If curiosity is about creating a short-lived knowledge gap, then mystery is an extended gap. It's a bit like a murder mystery where information gradually unfolds and you don't know the full picture until the end. It's probably one to use sparingly in business presentations but it can certainly be used.

So what? Over to you...

1. What emotional objectives are relevant to your presentation?

Begin powerfully

2. How will you achieve those objectives?

3. What's the best hook for your presentation?

Day 2
Reinforce ideas

Let's look now at a technique that's consistently underused in executive presentations: reinforcing ideas (the 'R' in the BRIBE acronym).

No audience will pay attention 100% of the time. Individuals are bound to drift, even if momentarily. 'Naked' presentations, without slides and other speaker support, are particularly challenging as audience retention can be as low as 10%.[4] Reinforce ideas to help listeners remember the important things you've said.

Clarify the core theme or message of your presentation, looking at the entire content of the presentation and summarizing it in a few words.

Repetition

Thankfully, there are other ways to repeat a core message. For example, putting a strapline on all slides in a deck works well; you can also show a video or written information that restates a key point.

Or you can highlight a single, significant item and repeat it, such as *Location, location, location* or *Education, education, education*. These are examples of repetition called *epizeuxis*, a technique that comes from Ancient Greek rhetoric.

The first example is the memorable title of a popular TV show in the UK and it's also a familiar phrase uttered by real estate agents. *Education, education, education* is taken from a conference speech by Tony Blair just before he became British Prime Minister. He was emphasizing his priority in government if elected. The speech is still remembered today and in particular those repeated words.

In the right place, this can be a potent technique, but use it sparingly.

Themes

To demonstrate this I sometimes use the words *hair*, *hairstyle* and *hairbrush*. People don't always remember

Reinforce ideas

all three words but they almost always remember the hair theme and a couple of the hair words.

Someone who uses themes brilliantly is research professor Brené Brown in her TED Talk 'The Power of Vulnerability'.[5] She argues that connecting deeply to ourselves and the world around us requires us to embrace our vulnerability in order to feel joy, gratitude and happiness. Disconnection, on the other hand, from pain in our lives creates many serious problems.

One of her early slides is a close-up of a child's hand protectively held in the palm of an adult. It's a tender image and portrays connection perfectly. Also it's hard not to notice the racial impact of the image. Both child and adult are black, and even in the 21st century this seems to stand out because the context is universal, not racial.

Another way Brown reinforces her theme is with storytelling. She relates an amusing first encounter between herself and her therapist. The story starts with struggle and resistance. Later she reveals that she had a breakdown before learning to lean into her own vulnerability.

The positioning of the story is effective in joining the two halves of the presentation. The story reinforces all the early points about understanding the concept of connection, and it also prepares the audience for the second half of the presentation, which focuses on solutions and how to achieve connection.

The news model

The structure of a news bulletin offers a simple template for where to reinforce ideas:

- Headlines
- Stories
- Break – recap or still to come
- Stories
- Recap

The headlines are similar to the introduction of a presentation. The headlines tell the audience the key stories in the bulletin. The introduction to a presentation lets the audience know the main themes.

Individual news stories are similar to key points in a presentation. They're the place where ideas are explained.

Halfway through a bulletin, audiences get a breather. The anchor either recaps the top stories or points to what's 'still to come'. That is, the anchor lets the audience know the main stories that will feature in the rest of the bulletin. Introducing a breather into presentations gives the audience an opportunity to process what they've heard and breaks up the pace of the presentation. It also gives the speaker an opportunity to restate the themes of the presentation.

The recap at the end of a bulletin gives the audience a final opportunity to hear what's going on in the world. The conclusion of a presentation gives the audience one last chance to understand the main points and ideas.

So... tell them what you're going to tell them, tell them, then tell them what you just told them.

Q&A

In the introduction to the Q&A you can remind an audience of the main points they've heard in the preceding presentation.

When taking questions there's a simple formula to make answers clear and emphatic: PEP.

P = the point that answers the question.

E = the example that explains the point.

P = the main point restated or summarized.

Use the conclusion of the Q&A as the last opportunity to reinforce your theme or key point.

The persuaders

Make use of persuasive words as you get your message across and reinforce your ideas. I call these *the persuaders*.

- Discovery
- Guarantee
- Love
- Proven
- Results
- Save
- Easy
- Health
- Money
- New
- Safety
- You[6]

So what? Over to you…

1. What's the theme of your presentation?

2. What points need repeating?

Reinforce ideas

3. What techniques will you use to repeat ideas?

Day 3

Involve the audience (and manage your script!)

This chapter looks at the 'I' in the BRIBE acronym that I introduced in the Day 1 chapter.

Speaker and audience must be involved to achieve success! Let's look at the techniques that really bring an audience into a presentation:

- Meaningful eye contact
- Content that doesn't overload an audience – Magic 7
- Clearly organized ideas using the pyramid structure
- Stories that connect audiences to the subject and the speaker

Involve the audience (and manage your script!)

Eye contact

This is probably the most powerful tool for involvement but speakers often feel uncomfortable looking directly at people in an audience. Direct eye contact in some cultures is perceived as disrespectful or hostile. Even within cultures that use very direct eye contact, if it's held for too long it can be seen as aggressive or intrusive.

The venue may also be an issue: in very large auditoriums the distance can make it virtually impossible to make real eye contact. As can reading scripts.

Let's look at some solutions for improved eye contact.

Eye contact: mind maps

Rather than reading word for word from a script, consider using a mind map as your prompt. Mind maps help us speak in a more relaxed, natural style that's highly engaging. I like the fact that they're quick and easy to prepare. They're also brilliant for adapting to last-minute time changes. If you suddenly find yourself with less speaking time, it's really easy to drop key points or examples.

You can use different software tools to write mind maps on electronic devices, including *Mindmeister* and *iMindMap*. Or you can simply use brightly coloured felt-tip pens, which can help you to process and internalize the content of your presentation.

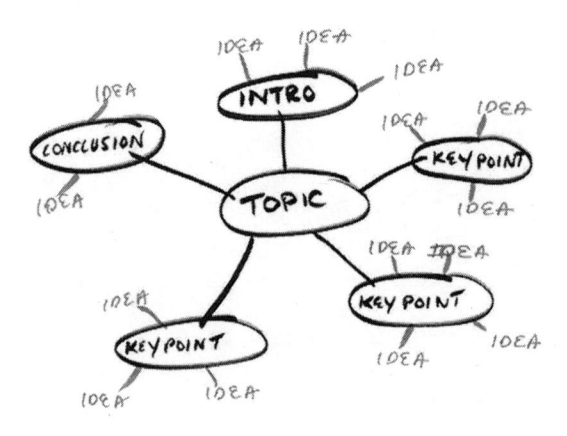

Fig. 3: Mind map

Let's say you have five elements to your presentation: introduction, three key points and a conclusion. Use a single word if possible as a prompt for your point.

If you're using a mind map as a speaker prompt, keep it really clear and easy to read so you don't have to look down for long. Rehearse it! You may discover

Involve the audience (and manage your script!)

some of the words you've chosen are not the best prompts for you for triggering the ideas you want to explain.

Tips

- Use capital letters – they're easier to read in a live presentation.
- Use just one or two words – too many words make the mind map cluttered and they're harder to remember.
- Use colour – a different colour for each key word and its supporting ideas helps you see how ideas are related at a glance.
- Draw simple images – a visual cue helps with remembering the point.
- Use delivery prompts – for example, an asterisk could signal the next slide, an exclamation mark could signal a pause.

Alternatively, you might prefer to work with bullet points on cue cards. Once again, you can use colour, capital letters, key words and wide spacing to help.

Overload: Magic 7

One of the best tools for keeping audiences involved is Magic 7, which prevents overloading the audience with information. It refers to a theory by psychologist George Miller often called *The Magical Number Seven, Plus or Minus Two*. He said that we can hold seven random items in short-term memory at any one time. That number can go up to nine or reduce to five.[7]

When we apply this idea to presentations, grouping ideas around seven key points works fine. If you want to be cautious, five key points avoids any chance of overload.

Clearly organized ideas: the pyramid structure

Barbara Minto's excellent *Pyramid Principle* is a tool for communicating ideas – when ideas flow well the audience stays with the speaker.[8]

The pyramid structure puts ideas into simple pyramids with a headline at the top and supporting points at the bottom of the pyramid.

See Figure 4 for my presentation titled 'How to Do a Great Presentation' in pyramid format. Note the second line below the title is called the keyline and it identifies the two main arguments of the

Involve the audience (and manage your script!)

presentation. In my case a great presentation is all about 1) the message and 2) the messenger.

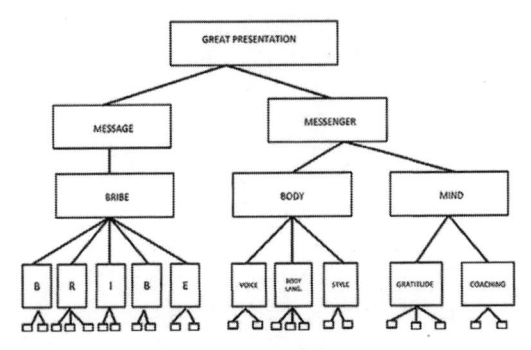

Fig. 4: Pyramid structure of 'How to Do a Great Presentation'

The keyline boxes answer the question implied by the box above:

- If the question is how do you do a great presentation, the answer is focus on the message and the messenger.
- If the question is what can a messenger do to achieve a great presentation, then the answer is pay attention to your body and your mind.
- If the question is how can your body help with a great presentation, the answer is work on your voice, your body language and your style.

- Any box in the pyramid explains the one above that it's linked to.

Stories that connect through storytelling

Once you've got the structure sorted it's time to make the content come alive. Here's the breakdown of a story I sometimes share when introducing myself to groups.

The beginning

The story is about an important moment in the life of a ten-year-old child. The story takes place in a classroom where a teacher asks various ten-year-olds to read out an assignment. One by one the children proudly read one or two pages.

The middle

The teacher asks the final child to read her story and quickly adds that she knows the child has written eight pages but there's only time for her to read out the first two pages. The child is confused and upset and dives under her desk.

Involve the audience (and manage your script!)

The end

I reveal that I'm the child, and I couldn't have known that moment was the start of something amazing in my life, that I'd grow up with a lifelong passion for communication that would influence every job I've done. With a clear communication theme established, I then describe a few significant jobs or roles I've done and weave them into the theme. It's a much more memorable and creative way of communicating biographical information.

Of course, not all stories have to be personal. You could describe a turning point in a project, an outstanding contribution, a dramatic moment, a sad moment, a funny moment. You get the idea.

Using the word *imagine* to start a story gets the brain all fired up waiting for what's next. Parables or stories from religious sources can also be used effectively in business presentations.

Scripts

I don't often use scripts when speaking but sometimes it's the best option. Let's look at the following techniques one by one:

- Rewrite
- Rehearse
- Mark up scripts
- Fine-tune
- What to do on the day
- Using smartphones and tablets

Rewrite

The goal is to get the script to sound as close as possible to your natural speaking voice.

Conference organizers once wrote a script for me to introduce the conference, welcome the guests and close the conference. The content was excellent but the language didn't sound like me so I needed to transform it into 'Jacqui speak'.

I shortened the sentences so they were easier to say and I changed words so the tone was more conversational. For example, the original script said:

Thank you to these incredible people, who are here today, for sharing their very personal stories.

The rewritten script was:

Such incredible young people. Thank you for sharing your stories. And it's great to have you here today.

Involve the audience (and manage your script!)

I used contracted versions of familiar phrases; for example, 'we are' was changed to 'we're'. I also used 'set-up' phrases to introduce important ideas before actually saying them. For example, 'I'd like to share a couple of important stats with you.' These cues help to prime the audience to pay particular attention.

Double line spacing makes a script so much easier to navigate in a live situation. It means when looking up and down from the script it's easy to find your place and keep regular eye contact with the audience.

I've occasionally seen speakers falter when their script pages come out of order. One solution is to staple the script pages or link them together with a treasury tag. But be aware that a sensitive mic will pick up the sound of the pages being turned.

You could also number the script pages (I'm talking numbers written in big, black felt-tip pen so you can see them at a glance, not tiny, printed ones at the bottom of the page). Once numbered, hold the pages together with a paper clip. At the podium remove the paper clip so you can slide the pages from right to left as you read.

Rehearse

I read the script all the way through – several times – so that I became comfortably familiar with it, but not to the point of knowing it by heart.

Mark up scripts

I then used annotations to enhance my presence and impact. My system includes underlining words that needed vocal emphasis, and I insert an asterisk where I want to remind myself to pause within a paragraph.

I circle an asterisk to prompt me to do a 'power pause' that separates one key idea from another (see also Day 6: Vocal presence). This not only allows the speaker to breathe but it also gives some space for the audience to process the information, and it signals to them that a new, important idea is about to begin.

I highlighted in yellow the names of the sponsors so their name checks were given sufficient vocal weight.

See Figure 7 for the first page of my conference script and the mark-up I did.

Involve the audience (and manage your script!)

ACTUAL SCRIPT — JH

Jacqui Speech

12.10

Welcome

~~Young people~~, Your Royal Highness, Lord Leftenant, Lord Mayor, Ladies and Gentlemen, Good Afternoon.

On behalf of Leeds Community Foundation and our sponsors DLA Piper, EY, Standard Life and Westfield Health, I'd like to welcome you here today to this very special event. We are proud and honoured that *His Royal Highness, Prince Henry of Wales,* is able to join us along with our other speakers. All share our vision of working together to end the stigma around mental health issues.

Before we get going, a little housekeeping information. There is no planned fire alarm test for today. If you do hear the fire alarm, please leave via the exits and wait at the assembly point in Bond Court. Also, now is the time to make sure your mobile phone is switched to SILENT - but do feel free to keep tweeting from the event. And the hashtag is #giveloveleeds.

SUPER PAUSE

I'd like to share a couple of important stats with you.

- **50%** of adult mental health problems start before age **15**
- and 75% before the age of 18.

Fig. 7: Jacqui script with mark-ups

Fine-tune

I fine-tuned the rehearsals to see what needed adjusting. I first recorded sound only to assess how fluently I came across and to gauge the expressiveness in my voice.

Then I watched vision only, with the sound muted, to check my body language, gestures, facial animation, etc.

In the last rehearsal I reviewed both sound and vision. By this time I was very happy and comfortable with the script.

I was able to do a full walk-through at the venue the day before. I used the opportunity to 'own the space'. This is a combination of breathing into the space, testing mics and walking to and from the podium.

What to do on the day

In the early morning I read through the scripts in private. The adrenaline always kicks in at this point!

And finally I focused on the start of the speech when the audience is most attentive and when the rapport between speaker and audience is established.

Involve the audience (and manage your script!)

Using smartphones and tablets

I've seen people speak effectively from scripts on their smartphones or tablets, but bear in mind that technology can let you down. Top tip: Make sure the display option on your device is set to 'always on' to avoid your script disappearing from the screen when you're in the middle of speaking!

So what? Over to you...

1. How might you use a mind map to help you deliver a more engaging presentation?

2. Try drawing out your presentation as a hierarchy: what do you notice?

Involve the audience (and manage your script!)

3. What personal (or other) story can you tell to introduce your topic more memorably?

Day 4

Be bold

Once in a while you'll get a speaker you just can't forget. Not a perfect speaker, but one who is truly present. The audience is immersed in a well-prepared presentation: result – an inspired audience and an opportunity realized. Let's now look at the second 'B' in the BRIBE acronym – Bold.

- Being bold is about being your best self in a presentation: authentic and fully present.
- Being bold is about investing the time to make your presentation fresh, interesting and engaging.
- Being bold is about doing presentations that make organizations better.

Being yourself

Being yourself in a presentation is probably one of the boldest things you can do, and few people manage it.

Show up authentically and wholeheartedly. That might not happen because of nerves or a sense of not being good enough. The solution lies in self-acceptance and self-awareness. Speakers who show up as fully themselves have a presence that tells the audience their presentation will be authentic and exciting.

Tell personal stories

Humour can be powerful. It can instantly transform the relationship of speaker and audience. The sharing of something funny binds two parties positively: people relax more and open up to each other. However, I usually caution against 'trying to be funny' unless you're skilled or naturally funny.

Instead, I encourage speakers to tell a personal story to bring light touches to their presentations. It can be a story of you getting things muddled. It can be a story that shows you don't take yourself too seriously. It can be a self-deprecating story. It can be amusing. It will be original material because it's from your life and not many people will have heard it. It will also provide insights about you to an audience.

Offer great graphics

So many people grind the audience down with text-heavy slides, but research indicates that graphics can dramatically increase retention.[9] Here are a few principles for making graphics work well for your audience:

- Relate to your graphics – love them!
- Less data is more.
- Avoid split focus.
- Use large fonts for important numbers.
- Include faces of people.
- Use high-contrast colours.

Documentary-style slides

Accomplished television anchors Peter Snow from the UK and Ann Macmillan from Canada did a presentation on their book *War Stories* in the style of a television documentary. They used well over 100 slides in their 30-minute, fast-paced, high-energy presentation, telling stories of individual war heroes with lots of photos and pictures of people, places, action and landscapes. It felt like voiceovers in a live documentary, although obviously we could see them on stage.

Use acronyms

These are quick, easy ways to remember ideas. I use BRIBE (see Day 1) to help participants remember my content model. It's effective because it brings together a wide range of ideas in an easy-to-remember format. Sometimes I support the acronym with an image, sometimes not.

Acronyms give speakers the opportunity to be creative and memorable with their messaging. Take the familiar letters 'BBC' (British Broadcasting Corporation). Using the acronym technique I can create an executive presentation using the same three letters but they stand for something entirely different.

If I was doing a short presentation on how to begin a speech powerfully, I could structure my content around the BBC acronym, denoting the following three points:

B – Body
B – Breath
C – Creativity

So, my presentation on how to begin a presentation powerfully could work something like this:

Element of the presentation	Letter of acronym	Description of content
Intro		This presentation shows you the 'BBC' model to start a speech with impact.
Key point 1	B – Body	How you use your body has an impact on your audience even before you start speaking. Focus on facial expression, gestures, posture, physical energy to give your presentation a strong start.
Key point 2	B – Breath	Breath. This section discusses diaphragmatic breath and how important it is for high-grade public speaking. I explain how to breathe with the diaphragm.
Key point 3	C – Creativity	Encourage speakers to lose their reluctance to be creative in executive presentations. Show compelling examples. The use of the acronym BBC in the presentation is itself a creative device.
Outro		Concluding remarks.

Fig. 5: BBC acronym

Be bold

The BBC acronym therefore has a useful structural function and provides a simple flow of ideas.

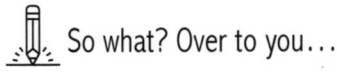

✏️ So what? Over to you...

1. What personal stories can you use to introduce or support your presentation?

2. How might you use visual content more effectively in your presentation?

Be bold

3. Have a go at using a well-known acronym to help you structure your key points. What do you notice?

Day 5
End powerfully

You're now reaching the end of your presentation (the 'E' in the BRIBE acronym). Here are the must-do things that apply to virtually all presentations.

- The flag – let the audience know the presentation is about to end.
- The review – recap key ideas from the speech.
- The call – let the audience know what action they need to take.
- The out – the device that actually ends the presentation.

Your ending needs so much attention. It's when the audience is highly attentive and what you say in the closing moments is most likely to be remembered.

End powerfully

Psychologists call it the *'Recency Effect'*: people recall items at the end more clearly than those at the beginning.[10]

I see a similar effect with presentations when I talk to delegates after a speech. It's very likely audiences will remember what you say at the end, so make it count. *'The flag'* is one way to do this.

The flag

To make the most of the Recency Effect, let audiences know the end is coming. One way to do this is to signal the end. You can do this with a slide but most people choose to do it with simple phrases. For example:

- 'To conclude my presentation...'
- 'To end, I'd like to leave you with...'

Don't underestimate the power of these phrases. Audiences may shift in body position and the energy level in the room surges. It's a good time to restate important ideas or key messages.

But there's a caveat: end must mean end. Don't use multiple flags – the audience won't thank you for it!

The review and the call

Review your presentation or summarize what you've said by including bullet points, mind maps, a graphic, a story or a quote. Make sure you keep the review clear and sharp and think about whether you want to summarize a single global point or a few key messages.

The 'call' is sometimes called the 'call to action'. It lets the audience know exactly what you want them to do next. Express the call clearly and explicitly.

The out

The 'out' is something special. It models the 'and finally' story in a news bulletin. The 'out' is the last thing an audience hears or sees: a question, a new thought, a new graphic, a plea, a gesture.

One I particularly like is an 'out' that references a point made at the beginning of a presentation. It can be something as simple as recalling an image, quote or item of data that started the presentation, to help the audience recall what's been said throughout the whole presentation, and to tie up the whole thing with a satisfying sense of closure.

End powerfully

So, give thought to the end of a presentation and make even the last seconds count. Be clear about what you want your audience to remember and the best way to do that.

So what? Over to you...

1. How do you usually finish presentations, and how might you change that?

2. What's the 'call' for your presentation, and how can you express it clearly at the end?

End powerfully

3. How might you create the 'out' to finish your presentation strongly?

Day 6
Vocal presence

Why vocal presence matters

Research by psychologists from the University of Glasgow powerfully demonstrates the need for strong vocal presence from the very first utterance in a presentation.[11] After hearing just the word 'hello', listeners decided on a speaker's personality. The personality traits they selected from included:

- Aggressiveness
- Attractiveness
- Competence
- Confidence
- Dominance
- Femininity
- Likeability

Vocal presence

- Masculinity
- Trustworthiness
- Warmth

The researchers concluded that the initial impression formed from hearing less than a second of sound of someone's voice was likely to be the same impression held after listening to the voice for a longer period. You only get one chance to make a first impression vocally.

Improving vocal presence helps achieve vocal attractiveness, varied pitch and the all-important trust. Strong vocal presence is critical in 'naked' presentations, where an executive isn't using any supporting visuals. It's also particularly important in audio conferences, phone meetings and webinars when the speaker isn't seen by the participants.

The first step in developing vocal presence is conducting a presence audit.

The presence audit

The presence audit describes who you want to be as a human being. I use the word 'audit' here because this activity is about data collection and evaluation for the purpose of future improvement – much like any other audit.

The presence audit has two stages:

1. Collect and evaluate data about presence.
2. Create a three-word report to drive your future improvement.

Presence audit: collect and evaluate data

It's time to reflect on your presentations, and here are some questions to ask yourself:

- Which have been my best presentations and why?
- Which presentations didn't go so well and why?
- How would I describe my presence in both cases above?
- How would I describe my presence today?

Brainstorm the answers that colleagues, friends and loved ones would give to the questions above. Ask them for their feedback on your presence.

The information gives a useful picture of how you're currently coming across in presentations. Now reduce the comments to single words.

Then stand in a place where you can see your future self excelling in so many ways when presenting. What words would capture that excellence? What words

Vocal presence

would describe your presence? Does your existing list contain the words or do you need to add words?

Presence audit: three-word report

The goal is to select three words from the data you've collected to capture the presence of the future, brilliant you.

So when you look at the words in your data collection, which seem most useful for you going forward as an executive presenter? Underline them. Now take a long, hard look at the words underlined and settle on three words.

Write them down. These words are like gold dust because they can help you lean into your future. Put them on your desktop, smartphone or fridge. Maybe even make them your new password! See them several times every day. High visibility will help embed them in your life and in your vocal presence.

Vocal competence

The presence audit gives us the foundation and framework for vocal competence. The areas of competence we look at are diaphragm breathing, resonance and fine-tuning the voice.

The voice is wonderfully unique. Yet it's remarkable that such a vital part of our identity and professional toolkit should be so underdeveloped.

When we are improving the voice, some of the activity is connected to the respiratory system, for example diaphragm breathing. Some activity is to do with the digestive system, such as articulation exercises using the lips, mouth and teeth.

Vocal competence: diaphragm breathing

To use the diaphragm effectively takes time and practice and sometimes feels counter-intuitive.

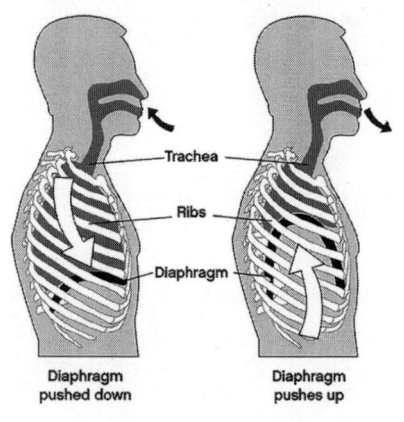

Fig. 8: Diaphragm breathing

Vocal presence

It can be quite straightforward to practise diaphragm breathing once you know the mechanics of breath. Figure 8 shows the diaphragm muscle located just underneath the lungs. The image on the left-hand side shows what happens when we breathe in air: the lungs expand and the diaphragm gets pushed down to allow the intake of as much air as possible. Then when we breathe out, the diaphragm pushes the air upwards as the lungs get smaller and air comes out of the mouth, as indicated in the image on the right-hand side.

The easiest way to practise diaphragm breathing is to lie on the floor and put your hands gently on your abdomen. Breathe in to the count of three and notice your abdomen rise. You've got it right when you breathe in and at the same time your stomach moves out. Now exhale over three counts. When you breathe out, your stomach should move inward, forcing the air out of the lungs with the help of the diaphragm muscle.

Put your hands around the sides of your ribcage. Breathe in deeply so your hands are pushed outwards. Release the breath. Make sure that you're not lifting your shoulders up, and if they become tense give them a shrug and a shake.

Now put your hands around your waist, breathe in and, as you breathe out, make a 'shhh' sound. As you breathe out feel the muscles around your waist and stomach moving inwards as they support the air out of your body.

When you're ready to progress, take in enough breath so you can breathe out on a count of five or more. To really activate the power of diaphragm breathing, practise increasing the out breath to at least 20 counts over two weeks.

Vocal competence: resonance

Resonance is the amplification of sound in our chest, throat and head. With regular exercises your voice can produce a rich sound that many people associate with gravitas.

The vocal cords (Figure 9) are located in the throat and consist of two folds that vibrate and elongate to produce sound. You can feel the folds vibrating if you gently hold your neck with one hand and hum. If you hum a high note the reverberation is less noticeable. If you go for a deeper note you can feel a longer elongation of the cord.

There are many ways to warm up the vocal cords, such as humming a tune.

Vocal presence

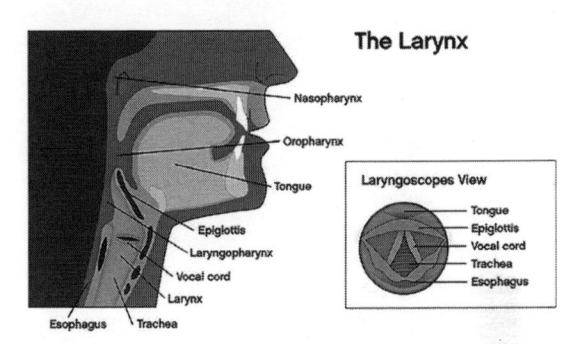

The Larynx

Fig. 9: Vocal cords

We now move from the throat to the head resonators: the tongue, lips and teeth, and soft palate.

The tongue plays a significant role in how the voice sounds. It's a strong muscular organ with a big digestive function of swallowing and pushing food around as we chew. For speech it functions best when relaxed at the root. These exercises will help reduce root tension. Try the following tongue movements:

- Move your tongue out and in then up, to the side, down and then to the other side.
- Now say out loud the following sounds. You'll notice that they really get the tongue working.

Ta ta ta ta

La la la la

Na na na na

Lily, Lily, Lily, Lily

Tell Terry Tucker and Tommy Tatler not to tell tales

Now the lips. The following exercises encourage the lips to move positions efficiently. The exercises also open and close the lips.

- Say the following out loud:

    Eee, ooo, eee, ooo

    Ma ma ma ma

    Pa pa pa pa

    Ba ba ba ba

    Mwa mwa mwa mwa

    Sweet Sue, sweet Sue

Now it's the turn of the soft palate. It's at the back of the roof of the mouth and consists of muscle and connective tissue. It helps to make most of the sounds

Vocal presence

of speech. A soft palate that's not working optimally makes speech sound nasal and weak.

You can wake up the soft palate with a simple yawn. How hard is that? Another exercise for the soft palate involves making sounds.

- Say the following out loud:

    Ka ka ka ka

    Ga ga ga ga

    Nga nga nga nga

    Kick cake and coke quite quickly

Vocal competence: fine-tuning

Now that we've got major muscles and resonators working, it's time to start fine-tuning and work with words. Tongue twisters are fantastic for speaking with clarity and precision. They're particularly helpful for executives speaking in a second language or addressing international audiences.

Tongue twisters

Say with as much clarity, passion and purpose as you can!

Red lorry, yellow lorry

Red leather, yellow leather

Rubber baby buggy bumpers

Now make it a little harder by saying it with the same precision but a little faster.

Placing meaning

Ensuring audiences understand the meaning and focus of our presentations is central to successful communication.

When teaching I get participants to work on poetry or dramatic speech. My INSEAD colleague Steve Knight reintroduced me to 'Invictus' by Victorian poet William Ernest Henley. Many people will associate the poem with the late President of South Africa, Nelson Mandela. He used the poem to keep his spirit alive when imprisoned on Robben Island. It's easy to see why he found the words so powerful and inspiring.

Here are two lines from the poem:

I am the master of my fate,

I am the captain of my soul.

Vocal presence

Part 1 of the exercise on placing meaning

To do the first part of this exercise, concentrate on the first line of the poem: 'I am the master of my fate'. Say the line out loud and, each time you say it, emphasize a different word as underlined in the following. Don't just say the words; express a really significant idea each time you say a line.

I am the master of my fate

I *am* the master of my fate

I am *the* master of my fate

I am the *master* of my fate

I am the master *of* my fate

I am the master of *my* fate

I am the master of my *fate*

Part 2 of the exercise on placing meaning

Now do exactly the same activity, but this time use a single sentence from a business presentation. Emphasize a different word each time you say the whole sentence.

The goal is to go into all presentations being intentional about the words you emphasize and how you shape meaning for your audience.

Practising vocal competence

I have three levels of practice: gold, silver and bronze.

Gold

Gold-level practice is achieved from daily work. It can be as short as five minutes each day doing three activities:

1. The first and non-optional activity is taking time to focus on diaphragm breathing.
2. Then choose one activity to improve the resonance of your voice and its gravitas. Hum a simple tune such as 'Happy Birthday' or your favourite song. This will gently warm up the vocal cords and prepare your voice for the work ahead.
3. Finally select one activity to fine-tune your voice. I'd go for power pauses that separate one idea from another. Read business stories with purpose and passion aloud from your smartphone. End each sentence with a power pause. Elevate the ideas with your delivery.

Vocal presence

Silver

Silver-level practice is regular practice but with less frequency, say every few days or once a week. You do one activity from each of the three categories: breathing, resonance and fine-tuning. It's still beneficial but won't achieve optimal results.

Bronze

Bronze-level practice is done on an ad hoc basis. An example of this would be doing three practice activities on the day of a presentation. It will still make a difference to your vocal presence.

One final item on how to increase the impact of vocal presence comes from voice coach Michaela Kennen. Her advice is to 'follow the full stop'.

'For a better voice, focus on ending sentences. Formulate ideas so you can use a proper downward inflexion to end sentences. Then your body can take a breath. Practise doing this at the beginning of a presentation so your body gets into the rhythm of landing an idea and taking a breath.'

✏️ So what? Over to you...

1. How can you incorporate practising diaphragm breathing into your life? How often can you do it?

Vocal presence

2. What would you like to develop in your vocal presence?

3. Which voice exercises are most relevant to you?

Day 7
Body language and style

Body language and your signature style can be a big help in communicating ideas and important information.

Body language to support speaker credibility

As soon as an audience sets eyes on a speaker, they're judging their personal qualities, competence and professionalism. Impressions formed in the first five seconds tend to be the same view held after a much longer period.[12]

Walk-on

With this five-second, first-impression window in mind, it's useful to focus on the way you walk to a podium to start a presentation. A brisk walk with energy, purpose and an upright posture commands attention and builds credibility.

If you think there's room for improvement in your walk-on, use rehearsal time to practise. Record yourself if at all possible. Pay attention to PPE: posture, pace and expression (facial).

Grounded posture

Adopting a grounded posture to start a presentation looks confident and facilitates gestures. A grounded posture means standing with your feet about hip-width apart with softly bent knees, an upright posture and hands loosely at the side.

Grounded posture can also boost the voice, provided the upper body is held upright with open shoulders. An upright body has the spine, back and head aligned. One way to achieve this is to imagine a piece of string starting from the base of the spine (the lower back) and coming out of the top of your head. Keep your spine, back and head in line with the imaginary string. The breath moves in and out more efficiently with this alignment, which in turn improves the sound of the voice.

It's possible, and a good idea, to maintain a grounded posture when sitting down to speak. Keep your feet flat on the floor and sit upright. Do not rest your body against the back of a chair – make sure you're supporting your spine solely from your seated position. Keep your shoulders open and align your spine, neck and head.

Hands behind the back

I've never been a fan of presenting with hands held behind the back and I encourage speakers not to begin their speech with this posture. Maybe it's the military association that troubles me. It feels overbearing and often looks awkwardly stiff.

Move with purpose

Move with purpose and make each movement tie into the structure of the presentation. For example, you might do the intro and first key point from centre stage; then the next key points at stage left and the subsequent key point stage right. You might choose to conclude by returning to centre stage position. This gives an evident point to movement.

With rehearsal it's straightforward to make the movements look poised, confident and professional.

Nerves

Nerves can overwhelm us and undermine credibility when speaking. At the same time, watching highly nervous speakers can be uncomfortable for an audience.

When nerves take over, a range of physical reactions are triggered. These include a faster heartbeat, rising blood pressure and perspiration. Tightness in the muscles in the neck and chest can make the voice wobble. Adrenaline rushes through the body.[13]

When in the grip of these reactions you do need rapid solutions to restore control. Slowing down the out breath and breathing deeply is a good place to start.

Reducing nerves with 'rag doll'

If nerves kick in well before you're on stage or in the board room, there's another useful technique called 'rag doll'. This looks ridiculous, so is best done in private, but it's guaranteed to help release tension in the body and enable you to control some of the physical symptoms of nerves.

- Stand with your feet hip-width apart.
- Keep your knees slightly bent and slowly bend over as if to touch your toes.
- Keep your hands and arms loose and shake your shoulders from side to side five to ten times (losing all stiffness in the body, hence rag doll).
- Stand upright slowly to avoid feeling dizzy.

Facial expressions

Audiences will look closely at the face of speakers. An expressive face can increase rapport when speaking but you need to be self-aware and not overdo it. A highly animated face can disconcert an audience. Conversely, a facial expression that's too controlled may hamper rapport.

Smile

When audiences see a speaker smile, they often respond by smiling themselves. They can't help it.

Why? Well, smiling is contagious. The part of the brain responsible for smiling is an unconscious automatic response area called the cingulate cortex. Numerous researchers have noted a mirroring effect where we automatically copy the facial expression of others we see.[14]

Smiling produces neuropeptides that reduce stress. The body relaxes and heart rate and blood pressure lower. The release of the neurotransmitters dopamine, endorphins and serotonin lift our mood.

A smile directly affects how an audience relates to a speaker. 'People respond to those who smile, and evaluate them differently and more positively than those who do not.'[15]

Part of that positive speaker perception includes feeling a greater sense of trust and liking for the speaker and perceiving the speaker as more competent.

Body language to increase the impact of a business message

In a presentation, gestures can help both audience and speaker.

This idea of gesture in spoken communication seems to be borne out when speakers try to restrict

Body language and style

gestures. They find it's more challenging than expected and requires a lot of practice. They may even find gesture restriction interferes with the flow of speaking. This may also be due to the fact that we start to use hand gestures as infants. By adulthood, gestures have been integrated into our personality and communication style.

I don't like to prescribe gestures because if a speaker finds certain gestures uncomfortable or unfamiliar they won't work well anyway, at least not initially. I do like people to be aware of the gestures they use when speaking and assess the effect on audiences. Are the gestures helping to draw attention to words and ideas? Are they clarifying meaning? Recording and reviewing a rehearsal is a good way to assess this.

As you watch your movements, you might want to note the kind of gestures you're using and their impact. The three significant gestures presenters use are illustrators, regulators and adaptors:

- Illustrators – amplify what's being said (hand gestures).
- Regulators – control the audience in some way (raising an arm to get an audience to be quiet).

- Adaptors – these are anxiety displacements – these movements, such as fiddling with a pen, reveal the emotions of the speaker.

Here are some common gestures used to increase impact in presentations:

- The give – open two-handed gesture signalling and seeking trust.
- The show – hands wide apart in a big upward gesture. Useful in big conferences for creating energy and excitement.
- The chop – hand(s) moving quickly in a downward slicing action. Emphatic gesture.
- Palm up – an open gesture commonly used when explaining ideas.
- Palm down – conveys authority.

Beware of the closed palm and pointing finger. Audiences often find it irritating and even aggressive.

You're not the only one communicating: audiences also send signals from their body language to a speaker. Positive signals include sitting upright, a nod, smile or consistent eye contact. Slumped posture, avoiding eye contact, shuffling or folded hands can be negative signals that you'd be wise to observe and respond to.

Body language and style

Your signature style

Clothes speak to an audience: they can generate positive impressions and perceptions of trust, likeability and competence in the critical early moments of a speech.

The sorts of things that can diminish the presence of a speaker are:

- Clothes that are way too tight.
- Baggy clothes that 'drown' the wearer.
- Over-long jacket sleeves touching the fingertips.
- Trousers so long they crumple unattractively at the feet.
- Colours (clothes, accessories) that overpower the speaker or are too pale and washed out.
- Too many competing colours (clothes).
- Make-up – overpowering or unflattering.
- Clothes that seem too young for the speaker.
- Clothes that seem to age the speaker.
- Too much jewellery.

Develop your own signature style. This means dressing to suit your personal colouring and body shape and at the same time communicating who you want to be.

The presence audit

Look back at Day 6 and the three-word summary you chose to describe your ideal presence. Then ask yourself how effectively your appearance reflects that. Use it to help you dress authentically and to manage your appearance.

Defined style principles and qualities

Use style icons to identify the principles and qualities of your own signature style. Consider people whose style of dress you admire. They may be people you know, business executives or celebrities. There will be something about them that speaks to some aspect of your sense of self: your values, your style, your age, your work, etc.

Colour confidence: colour types (light, deep, warm and cool)

There's no doubt in my mind that some groups of colours look much better on people than others. The colours you wear *do* interact with your overall personal colouring and *do* get noticed by an audience, so keep an open mind about adopting a colour palette based on personal colour types.

Body language and style

For the purposes of clarity and easy understanding we'll work with four colour groups:

- light cool (LC)
- light warm (LW)
- deep cool (DC)
- deep warm (DW)

Light or deep?

It's usually straightforward to know whether you have overall light or deep (darker) colouring. Look closely in the mirror in natural daylight to assess the combined colour effect of your hair, eyes and skin. Is it light or deep?

Warm or cool?

If you decide your personal colouring is *light* then the next thing to figure out is whether that lightness is more warm coloured or cool coloured. If you decide your personal colouring is *deep*, you also need to work out whether you fall into *deep and cool* (DC) or *deep and warm* (DW). When you look at your face and inside wrists do you see warm or cool undertones?

Ask people who know you to help if it's not immediately clear. Here are the colours you might want to consider trying to complement each colour type.

Colour group	Colour
LC (light cool)	Bright navy, charcoal blue grey, soft white, clear taupe, medium grey, pastel pink
LW (light warm)	Medium navy, peach, soft white, beige, ivory, cocoa, light warm grey
DC (deep cool)	Black, charcoal grey, dark navy, pure green, pure white, icy pink, icy blue
DW (deep warm)	Chocolate brown, rust, camel, teal, orange, olive green, beige, ivory, cream

Fig. 10: Colour groups and palettes

The colour groups are related to the palettes because they share the same properties. For example in the group *deep cool* (DC) the palette contains colours that are themselves deep and/or cool.

If you feel a colour is somehow integral to your personality, you'll feel great when you wear it, so it may well have a place in your signature style. Consider getting a second opinion of the colour from a trusted friend.

Colour confidence – colour combinations

Once you have a palette of colours that suit you, try using a colour wheel to help you work out new

Body language and style

colours that mix well together. It's literally a circular chart with 12 colours side by side: primary colours (red, yellow, blue), secondary colours (orange, green, violet) and tertiary colours (yellow-green, blue-green, blue-violet, red-violet, red-orange, yellow-orange).

The colour wheel helps you work out new colours that mix well together. The mixes are created by the position of colours on the wheel. See some of the mixes below.

The monochromatic mix

This refers to colours in the same column in the wheel: they're different shades of exactly the same colour. An example of dressing this way is wearing a pale blue shirt and mid-blue trousers. The monochrome look is good for business casual. It smartens up the look and comes across as 'pulled together'.

The analogous mix

Analogous just means similar so these colours are next to each other on the wheel either as pairs or as groups of three. Colours in this mix blend really well. The impact is harmonious and confident and stronger than the monochromatic mix.

The complementary mix

These colours are opposite each other on the wheel and create a vivid, contrasting effect. This mix is good for standing out from the crowd, for being bold.

The triadic mix

This is the combination of three colours that are evenly spaced around the colour wheel. For example, yellow, orange and pink (one space apart) or violet, orange and green (three spaces apart). This mix is for high-impact dressing.

Neutrals

The neutrals are black, navy, grey, brown, cream, white. They mix well with any of the colours in the wheel and also with each other. They're popular colour combinations for business as they look chic and professional. They say 'I am serious', but if overused can look a little boring or anonymous.

Body shape

The final component of a signature style is body shape. This means knowing your body shape and wearing styles to suit your shape. Be really honest with yourself about how you look *today*.

Body language and style

We'll work with four body shapes (regardless of gender):

1. Upright triangle
2. Inverted triangle
3. Straight
4. Large

Body shape	Characteristics in men	Characteristics in women
Upright triangle ▲	Shoulders narrower than hips	Hips wider than shoulders
Inverted triangle ▼	Shoulders wider than hips	Bigger shoulders than hips Large bust and narrower hips
Straight ▮	Hips and shoulders are similar width	Hips and shoulders are similar width Body shape doesn't come in at the waist
Large ▪	Typically more contoured shape than angular Waist can be the widest part of the body	Waist is the widest part of the body Hips and shoulders are similar width Can be curvy shape

Fig. 11: Body shapes

Image professionals help clients look great by assessing body shape and using balancing techniques to highlight strong body features and diminish the impact of weaker features.

The visual check

For a business presenter, the purpose of completing a visual check is to feel confident that their appearance is well-presented and consistent with their signature style.

Do your visual check in the actual clothes you intend to wear for a presentation and in front of a full-length mirror. Scrutinize your appearance and address any details that might detract from your presentation. The sort of details that might need attention include untidy hair, creased clothes, loose threads or dirty shoes.

Posture

My final point on signature style is the importance of good posture. Good posture includes holding an upright frame with shoulders open and down, and a straight spine – regardless of whether you're standing or

Body language and style

sitting. Poor posture can't help but undermine your presence.

Headshots

So you've worked hard on honing your body language, style, colour matching and posture: what next? Taking a professional headshot!

Many presentation situations actually require headshots. Participants often go online to look up information about those speaking.

Given that headshots are so widely used it makes sense to use pictures that exude executive presence.

Up-to-date headshots that come across well will help achieve a positive first impression to people who don't know you. That becomes even more important when we consider that the initial impression from photos can correspond closely with how you're perceived after an audience has actually met you.

I recommend investing in professional headshots taken by an experienced photographer. Indeed, there are now several companies who specialize in professional headshots for LinkedIn profiles and other business needs.

Preparing for a photoshoot

I recommend doing a presence audit to guide a photographer to take pictures that represent you positively, authentically and in a way that's consistent with your three-word audit.

In addition to the audit it's worth reviewing your signature style before meeting a photographer, to help guide decisions on clothes, accessories and personal grooming.

I wanted several images from my photoshoot as I needed a variety of headshots to use across online platforms, including blogs, website, LinkedIn and X/Twitter. (It's also better value to get several images from one photo session.) I drew up a headshot list:

1. Smart: fresh and relaxed
2. Smart: corporate and interesting
3. Smart: vibrant
4. Relaxed: informal

The headshot list was for my own purposes, but I did show the photographer a sample of five different headshots I'd researched from the internet that I thought worked well and that gave the photographer a feel for what I wanted to achieve.

Body language and style

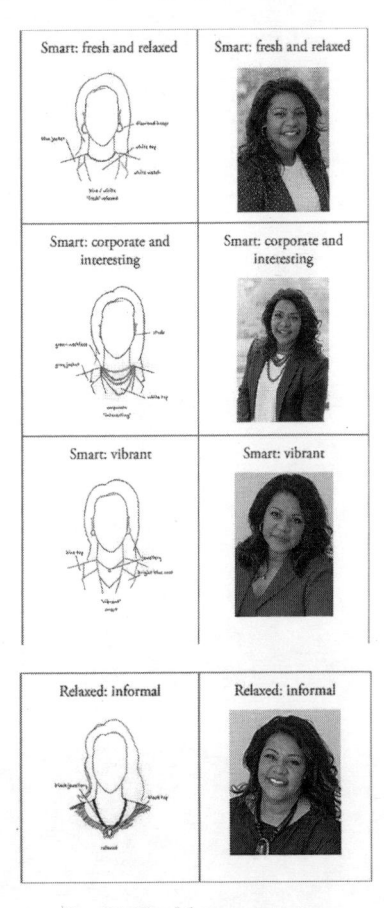

Fig. 12: Headshots comparison

✏️ So what? Over to you…

1. What unconscious gestures do you use? Ask others to tell you if you don't know!

Body language and style

2. What's your signature style, and how can you make it work for you?

3. What do your headshots say about you?

Day 8
Gratitude

Practising gratitude has been described as 'the ultimate performance-enhancing substance!'[16]

Let's now look at:

- How gratitude helps nerves.
- How gratitude improves personal presence.
- How gratitude helps connection.
- Ways to practise gratitude.

A few questions for you to consider as a speaker:

- Do you have a positive presence?
- Do you feel calm when addressing an audience?
- Do you feel happy?
- Do you manage your nerves well?

- Do you feel resilient to cope with the unexpected?
- Do you connect well with your audience?

I hope the answer is yes to all the above but, if not, the attitude of gratitude might be a solution – it can help a speaker to conquer nerves, develop a positive presence and connect well with an audience.

My interest in gratitude was inspired by my INSEAD colleague, Steve Knight, who uses it to develop vocal power. I always thought of gratitude as some sort of religious practice or philosophical pursuit – and of course it is! But it wasn't immediately clear to me that specific activities expressing gratitude would ever help anyone giving executive presentations.

Being grateful leads to a sense of well-being, feeling happier, being calm, feeling resilient and better social interaction. Indeed, it seems that these benefits can also be long-lasting.

Technological developments in neuroscience (particularly the use of the fMRI scanner) are also giving new insights into gratitude. It seems the brain has a distinctive area of its own that functions when we express gratitude, and that the positive effects of expressing gratitude can last weeks or months.[17] This is all compelling information about the value of practising gratitude for business leaders.

Gratitude helps nerves

'Help me get rid of nerves!' This crops up frequently on the wish-list of my workshop participants, and they often raise their eyebrows when I suggest that expressing gratitude can help control nerves.

When it comes to high-stakes presentations I get nervous like everybody else, but if I express gratitude it does cut down those nerves. In practice this means I tell myself *why* I'm grateful to be doing a particular presentation. It could be that I'm grateful to help others find their voice, or for the opportunity to learn from my talented audience.

Before a presentation I usually think these things in my head and that's often enough to calm me down. If I'm particularly anxious, I might state out loud my gratitude. If I'm feeling extremely challenged, I write down what I'm grateful for, which helps to shift focus away from internal anxiety and turns it into a potentially positive outcome.

Gratitude helps presence

Our presence is obviously affected by our mental and physical health and practising gratitude can contribute to both. Let's start with the benefits to mental health described in one study.

Participants who took part in gratitude research were asked to write letters of gratitude. They reported developing a significantly more grateful disposition two weeks after the task. They also reported feeling better mental health 4–12 weeks after they finished the task of writing a daily gratitude journal for 21 days.[18]

Gratitude can help with connection

Neuroscientists say that expressing gratitude generates activity in a specific area of the brain that has a small overlap with empathy and altruism.[19] That physical closeness perhaps explains why the act of gratitude increases our empathic behaviour. The Kini *et al.* research concludes that gratitude enhances empathy and affects our interactions with other people in that we're 'more willing to act in a way that has a positive impact on others'.[20]

Researchers call the increased connection with colleagues that comes with gratitude 'prosociality'. It means that people with a strong practice of gratitude have the capacity to be more empathic and to understand the perspective of others. They're also described as more generous and more helpful by people in their social networks.[21]

Ways to practise gratitude

Saying a prayer is one form, as people of faith have done for hundreds of years. But other ways to practise include:

Self-talk

I often say to myself the specific things I'm grateful for before a challenging presentation. Sometimes this is in the preparation phase and sometimes it's just before I speak at an event.

Gratitude journal or letter

Try journalling or writing gratitude letters – research has shown these to be particularly effective. Try a 21-day gratitude challenge – take the opportunity each day to reflect on the things you're grateful for.

Gratitude app

There are so many gratitude apps. Enjoy browsing to find one that works for you.

Gratitude meditation

There are loads of apps and sites that can assist with this. A great one is the ten-minute guided meditation I downloaded by Dr Kathi Kemper at Ohio State University's Center for Integrative Health and Wellness. It's designed to promote resilience through heart-centred gratitude: https://wexnermedical.osu.edu/~/media/Files/WexnerMedical/Patient-Care/Healthcare-Services/Integrative-Medicine/MP3-Files/Heart-Centered-Practices/Gratitude-2.mp3?la=en

So what? Over to you...

1. What three things are you grateful for right now?

Gratitude

2. How might practising gratitude help your presentations?

3. Which gratitude practice will you try out?

Day 9
Self-coaching

Is there something holding you back from excelling in your presentations? If so, self-coaching may help.

Mike Normant has developed an impressive self-coaching programme called *'Coach Yourself Up'*, which I'll reference several times in this section.[22] I recommend starting a journal to record answers to the questions in the exercises below. Your journal is also a good place to notice patterns of behaviour and track progress.

Before you start, it's also worth reviewing your presence audit to make sure it still reflects exactly who you want to be as a leader. If you haven't done one yet, do any of the words below belong in your presence audit?

Creative	Confident	Dynamic	Inspiring
Engaging	Authentic	Visionary	Clear
Decisive	Approachable	Articulate	Warm

Use your presence audit to guide your development as you go through the self-coaching exercises. NB: Coaching is not a quick fix and it will take practice to get close to your goal.

Managing attention

When you have more awareness of your attention, it increases your presence. It deepens the connection to self and to colleagues and makes for highly effective executive presentations.

Cultivating this superpower is challenging with constant distractions and interruptions occurring throughout the working day. Here are some ideas to help.

Exercise 1: Notice attention

Sit still for 30 seconds. Keep your eyes open. Where does your attention go? Let it go wherever it wants.

Self-coaching

Exercise 2: Direct attention

Now you need to learn how to *direct* attention.

Listen to a recording by Gary Sherman: www.mechanicsofawakening.com/free-downloads.html[23]

In the activity you focus attention for about ten seconds. This might be challenging at first.

Exercise 3: Direct your own attention

Sit still for one minute. Focus your attention on your mind for about ten seconds and then shift attention to your body and then to the world around you. Then go back to your mind, body and world – each time for approximately ten seconds.

Try it a few times.

Developing attention develops self-awareness. You become more aware of when your attention moves away and when you need to guide it back.

Exercise 4: Meditation

Meditation could aid your progress in managing attention. I encourage you to try it for two weeks – try starting your working day by relaxing and 'tuning in' to yourself. Try www.headspace.com.

Exercise 5: Single tasking

Watch the short five-minute video called 'Single Tasking is the new Multitasking' (less than five minutes long): https://www.youtube.com/watch?v=KzbxpzKwDXA which is about focusing attention on only one task at a time. When preparing presentations, single tasking could help get more done more efficiently.

Self-awareness

Let's now turn to personal stories and beliefs. These define how we see ourselves and the ways we behave that may stop us being fully present and effective speakers.

Ask colleagues, friends and loved ones about things you do habitually when presenting that don't serve you well. Show them the following list of self-limiting behaviours to see if they've noticed any of them in you:

- Not listening to feedback.
- Not implementing feedback.
- Not doing enough preparation and leaving it to the last minute.
- Over-preparing (rare!).

Self-coaching

- Not speaking clearly.
- Not speaking loudly enough.
- Speaking with a monotone voice.
- Speaking too quickly.
- Not looking at the audience.
- Not working on building rapport with an audience.
- Not smiling when presenting.
- Not pausing enough when speaking.
- Always dreading presentations.
- Not rehearsing important presentations.
- Never feeling confident doing presentations.
- Blaming others when presentations go wrong.
- Not communicating with your body.
- Gripping tightly onto a podium.

Exercise 6: Self-limiting behaviours

1. Write down all the self-limiting behaviours that you do.
2. Review input from friends and colleagues.
3. Identify the most significant behaviour for you.

Write down one you'd love to change and then rewrite it in an aspirational way, for example:

1. Self-limiting behaviour: I speak too quickly.

2. First draft of goal: I want to speak more slowly.
3. Rewritten aspirationally: I speak engagingly to colleagues/audiences.

Over the next few weeks start noticing the self-limiting behaviour you identified.

- How often does it occur over a day or week?
- How much time is there between its occurrence and when you notice it? (The belief is that the more you notice your self-limiting behaviour, the shorter the time between occurrence and awareness.)

More time spent 'noticing' your self-limiting behaviour often increases the chance of actually succeeding in changing the behaviour.

Getting to know our beliefs

The self-limiting things we do are generated from emotions, which themselves are generated from beliefs. Executive coaches often use the 'Ladder of Inference' to help clients understand their behaviour.[24]

Using the image of a ladder, at the bottom is observable data (things we see) and at the top is the action we take to respond to that data (our behaviour). Without realizing it, quite a lot happens between

Self-coaching

seeing something happen and responding to it. We filter the observed data and then we add meaning to that filtered data. We then make assumptions based on the meaning we created, and draw conclusions and check our adopted beliefs about the world before taking action based on those beliefs.

LADDER OF INFERENCE

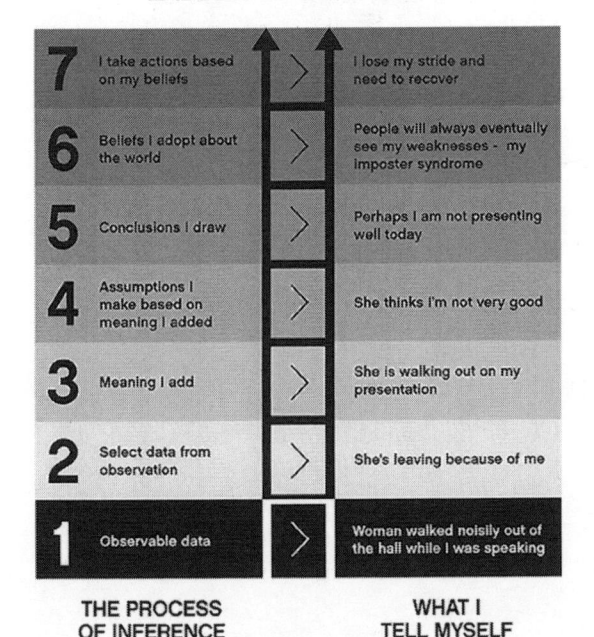

#	The Process of Inference	What I Tell Myself
7	I take actions based on my beliefs	I lose my stride and need to recover
6	Beliefs I adopt about the world	People will always eventually see my weaknesses – my imposter syndrome
5	Conclusions I draw	Perhaps I am not presenting well today
4	Assumptions I make based on meaning I added	She thinks I'm not very good
3	Meaning I add	She is walking out on my presentation
2	Select data from observation	She's leaving because of me
1	Observable data	Woman walked noisily out of the hall while I was speaking

Fig. 13: The Ladder of Inference

I once gave a speech in which a woman suddenly got up and left the hall. I felt anxious and momentarily lost my stride. In terms of the Ladder of Inference, I started at the bottom of the table in the box titled 'Observable data'.

After the speech I learned that the woman's departure had nothing to do with me: she was leaving early for childcare reasons. My worry was completely unnecessary; the story/belief controlling my behaviour was that I was an imposter and not 'good enough'.

Exercise 7: Challenge beliefs

Think of a presentation where something didn't go so well. Write down an outline of the event in your journal.

Now try to break down the event using the stages of inference. Capture it in the form of a table as above – peeling away all the layers of thinking until you see clearly the belief that's getting in your way. What have you learned from doing this activity?

Challenge your beliefs

Hopefully you're starting to identify beliefs that are getting in your way. If you're still thinking it over and

Self-coaching

could use some suggestions, have a look at this list of just a few of the stories/beliefs I hear frequently in my work as a communication coach:

- You're born with the ability to present.
- You can't get rid of nerves.
- I'll always hate presenting.
- I'm not an extrovert.
- I'm not a performer.
- I always beat myself up after a presentation.
- I can't speak in front of an audience.

The next step is to challenge your story by asking yourself the following series of useful questions to interrogate a self-limiting belief. I used them to challenge my belief that 'people will always see my weakness – my imposter syndrome'.

Crucial conversation questions

- What specific feelings connect to this story? (Be as precise as you can.)
- What evidence is there to support this story?
- Am I stepping into the role of victim/helpless person?
- What's my contribution to this story?
- What do I really want?
- What would I do if I really wanted these results?

Say your name!

Mike Normant also suggests using your *name* in the question so you address yourself in the third person ('What does Jacqui really want?'). It's based on research that indicates we can be more successful when dealing with our emotions when we use language that makes us a more detached observer.[25]

Exercise 8: Challenge stories

Practise interrogating your stories with any of the techniques above (Ladder of Inference, crucial conversation questions or say your name questions). Write down your answers. What did you notice as a result of the exercise?

Mental rehearsal: what is it?

Mental rehearsal is thinking through your performance, moment by moment, experiencing it in your mind as vividly as possible.

A good way of understanding how mental rehearsal affects performance is a computer analogy where software is the mind and hardware is the body. The software controls how well the hardware operates. Elite athletes have high-performing software that helps them use their hardware to the best of its ability.[26]

Self-coaching

It's thought that mental rehearsal fires the same brain cells that are actually involved in doing an activity, whether it's sport or communication.

It could be said that executives delivering high-stakes presentations face some of the challenges of elite performers. When delivering important messages, executives need to be confident, focused, highly motivated and highly engaged while under pressure – much like professional athletes.[27]

Three ways to do a mental rehearsal

The mental rehearsal can be done a couple of days before a big presentation, on the day of a major presentation or even just a few minutes before. Experiment to find what works best for you after looking at the three methods below.

Mental rehearsal – method 1

1. Choose a space where you won't be disturbed and where you can lie down or rest comfortably.
2. Close your eyes and relax your body. Start to focus your mind inwards.
3. Breathe in deeply and breathe out slowly. On the out breath start to release stress from your body. Focus on your feet first, then legs,

Present Like a Pro

then chest, then the top of your head. It's time to remove all distractions and let your mind relax.

4. Once relaxed, gently turn your attention to the presentation.
5. Speak to your mind. Mentally tell yourself that you're confident and that you can do a successful presentation. With self-confidence, repeat to yourself several times that you *will* succeed.
6. Imagine, in as much detail as you can, what you'll see just before you begin presenting. Visualize yourself actively engaged in speaking to an audience. Imagine that you're actually standing at the podium rather than watching yourself from the gallery.
7. Remaining relaxed and focused, mentally rehearse a successful presentation. Imagine going through the whole process and seeing highly successful results.
8. Repeat the previous step several times.
9. Finally, open your eyes and smile brightly. You've successfully performed a presentation in your mind, which is great preparation for an actual speech. I'm sure you'll now feel more confident in performing successfully

in the real presentation. Remember to praise yourself for being successful, as self-reinforcement is an important key to self-motivation.[28]

Mental rehearsal – method 2

1. Focus on the aspects of your presentation that you really want to do well.
2. Emphasize the *feeling* of presenting by referencing all the senses you can (see, hear, touch, taste, smell).
3. Create that image several times.
4. Imagine everything around you, including the conference hall, stage, podium, etc.
5. Include strategies for highly successful presentations in the image.
6. Finish with positive self-talk.

Mental rehearsal – method 3

Try using a script to talk out loud – one that gives a highly detailed account of the event you're preparing for. You could record the script and play it back while relaxing.

Here's a copy of an imagery script from the American fitness assessment programme for push-ups. After completing the mental rehearsal, soldiers do their actual fitness assessment.

> *You are standing in line for the push-up event. The air is crisp and smells of freshly cut grass. The temperature is cool.*
>
> *Your arms are strong and you are ready. You take in a slow deep breath, in to the count of five and out to the count of five.*
>
> *You are called up to begin the push-up event. You get down into the front-leaning rest position. The grass is moist and soft.*
>
> *You position your hands comfortably and wait for the start.*
>
> *You hear ready on the right, the right is ready; ready on the left, the left is ready. Ready – begin. Down and up, your arms feel strong and you are confident. Your form is good. You hear 1 minute has elapsed. Your arms are strong and steady and you are near your goal. You hear 30 seconds remaining. You continue up and down, breathing in on the way down and out on the way up. The final 10 seconds count down begins and you push out a few more. The event is over; you have done your best.*[29]

Self-coaching

Exercise 9: Mental imagery script

Now write your own imagery script for a presentation, incorporating the kind of ideas and detail in the military example above.

So what? Over to you...

1. What strong beliefs do you have about yourself as a presenter?

2. What do you fear most about speaking?

Self-coaching

3. What's your first step in self-coaching?

Day 10

Nerve management, and solutions

How do I manage my nerves? More people ask me this than anything else.

In addition to my own tips on nerves, I've included ideas from several top professionals below. I'm so grateful to them for sharing their experiences so generously.

Nerves often occur when a speaker is under-prepared or 'winging it'. Time is often a challenge in our busy lives, but successful leaders always invest time in preparing presentations.

Nerves can be a good indication of being in a focused and alert state ahead of a presentation. The problem starts when nerves overwhelm a speaker and get in the way of communication. When this happens, pay attention to breathing. If it becomes rapid and shallow, bring it under control. Slow down and breathe deeply. Pay attention to tense areas of your body and try to release some of the tension. Spend a minute or so beforehand doing a mental rehearsal. See yourself getting your message across successfully. Hold that feeling as you prepare to speak.

Preparation, preparation, preparation!

Rutger Schellens, CEO, ABN AMRO Clearing Bank

- If you are prepared the nerves are manageable.
- I keep my diary free the hour before a presentation to do last minute adjustments.
- I also schedule two hours for preparation two days before. That time is protected to allow me to get prepared.
- The time you spend on a business presentation beforehand makes a lot of difference in terms of nuance. It helps get the right words especially if content is more personal.
- I did a TED-style talk recently. I started work on it three to four weeks beforehand.

- The preparation for that included keeping sentences short and taking a break after each sentence.
- I was speaking to an audience of 300 people so I also practised delivering each sentence personally to a single person and the next sentence to a different person. It helped to focus on the text and the audience.
- My overall process of preparation is to focus on the storyline, fine tune then cut off. None of this is done the day before.
- One way to get rid of nerves is to share what you're feeling with the audience.

Tell stories

Paul Abrahams, Head of Corporate Communications, RELX GROUP

- Focus on storytelling if you're nervous about doing a presentation. Tell stories to connect at an emotional level. You want the audience to relate to you.
- Take the audience on a journey with you through your presentation so when you get to the call to action the audience think 'I like this

Nerve management, and solutions

person, I've listened to what they have to say and now they've asked me to do something – why wouldn't I do that?'
- Nerves can make people spend a lot of time on content but then they go off piste straight out of the gate. I remember one executive who did this and he never went back on piste and his credibility was damaged.
- Some people are naturally good at communication but it's something you can learn. There are techniques to help the message and body language, positioning, voice, cadence and timing.

Four strategies for nerves

Jeff Grout, Motivational Business Speaker, author and expert on people and performance

- The first point is authenticity. Being comfortable in your own skin helps effective communication yet so many people try to wear another skin.
- It's also about being comfortable in your own language. Often people feel compelled to use management speak or business speak instead of plain speaking.

- When I'm teaching groups and we come to the topic of nerves, people find it reassuring to know *everyone* in the group has a level of anxiety. Even people who seem 'natural' at public speaking are just better at hiding nerves.
- Nerves come from adrenaline and you need a certain amount to perform so it's a matter of managing them. The time to feel nervous is when you don't feel nerves.
- My nerves start 10–15 minutes before I speak. I get butterflies. Within two minutes those butterflies are in formation.
- Understand how your nerves are displayed. Often it's inside your body and not obvious to other people.
- If your nerves are transmitting externally, have a coping strategy. I know I will get dry mouth so I have water everywhere: at the lectern, stage right and stage left.
- Nerves also come from our inner voice. It can be our biggest critic or best advocate.
- When I am training leaders I ask them to bring draft scripts of their presentation. The first thing I ask them to do is to change all commas and semi-colons into full stops.

That immediately creates short sentences that are easier to deliver well and it makes speakers pause.

Interact

Brenda Ross, Executive Coach specializing in Leaders in Transition, Brenda Ross Associates

- Start with something interactive. It could be a comment or a question to do with getting to the presentation or about what it's like being there.
- The goal is to get the audience doing something: either saying something back to you, raising their hands or nodding their heads.
- Speak in a conversational tone to the audience and get them to interact before the presentation actually starts. This helps develop connection to the audience. It also means you've heard your voice so you feel less nervous. It breaks the silence and expectation that can weigh heavy at the start of a presentation and it helps you feel grounded.

Focus

Michaela Kennen, Voice and Dialect Coach

- Focus on what you can control in a presentation. You can control what you know, your arguments, how much you care about the subject and your outcome.
- When nervous, our breathing speeds up and we get a running breath. This is when you need to focus on sentence structure. Put a mental full stop and breath between sentences.
- If you are in a private space take in a breath through the nose and let go of the muscles in the tummy area or shoulders. Breathe out through the mouth. Focus on the 'out' breath. Breathe out longer and slower than the 'in' breath.
- If people can see you seated around a table or on a panel try this quick fix. Breathe in through the nose and on the slow out breath make a silent 'ff' sound. Do this several times to restore control.
- Remember that breathing alone cannot rescue a presentation that lacks clarity, preparation and rehearsal.

Nerve management, and solutions

Anti-nerve technique

Graham Davies, Presentation Coach

- The key to conquering nerves is to change your vague, negative thoughts into specific positive thoughts.
- In the last few hours before the speech, keep thinking about all the work you have done to prepare a brilliant script. Allow yourself to be proud of it.
- In the last five minutes before you are on, focus on just one thing: the first line of your script. Keep repeating the line in your mind.
- Keep your thoughts focused relentlessly on your first words, your mind does not have the energy to feel nervous as well.

Outside in: Use image

Jennifer Aston, Image Coach

- You build confidence from the inside out, but you can also help to build it from the outside in.
- If you look the part it helps you feel confident because people respond to you the way you

want. Use your image to trigger how you expect to be treated.
- When doing workshops I sometimes give a male participant a pair of slippers to wear. Eventually I ask how he felt dressed in business clothes and slippers. The reply is always that he felt disadvantaged the whole way through. What you wear will affect you internally as well as the message you give.
- When you're appropriately dressed you get the response you want from people.

So what? Over to you...

1. How do nerves impact you when it comes to presentations?

Nerve management, and solutions

2. What technique from this chapter will you try first, and why?

3. How might you 'build confidence from the outside in'?

Conclusion: My top ten tips

1. *Pay attention to recovery.*
   Go into a presentation expecting *something* unexpected to happen. The aim is not to deliver a perfect presentation, but to deliver the best presentation you can in the circumstances.

2. *Make the most of Q&A.*
   Invite questions from your audience and also ask them questions. Anticipate likely questions. Think about worst-case questions and how you want to approach them.

3. *Face the discomfort of difficult messages.*
   As you work out what to say in your presentation and how you'll say it, pay attention to how you're feeling. What level of discomfort are you feeling ahead of the presentation? What's driving the discomfort? Do you want to share your feelings with the

audience? Is it appropriate to do so? When you start speaking, observe the evident feelings of the audience. Try to connect with where they're at in what you say and do.

4. *Do your best with last-minute presentations*.
   The focus is on what can be done in the time available. Keep in mind the purpose of the presentation and what the audience specifically want or need from the speaker.

5. *How to present in a second language*.
   Start by accepting that the presentation might not be as good as mother-tongue presentations. But you can still do well if you prepare a lot more than you usually do. In addition to planning the content, plan the words you need and focus on vocabulary you don't know that will help.

6. *Keep to time*.
   Place a watch or a small clock in front of you so you can see time passing and how close you are to your ideal time. That way you can take your time if you're ahead and cut out things if you're behind. Rehearsing is necessary to keep to time.

Conclusion: My top ten tips

7. *Go naked!*
   'Naked' presentations are when speakers communicate without the usual trappings of slides. Ideas have to be clearly expressed so that comprehension feels effortless for the audience. The impact comes from using enriched language: stories, similes, metaphors and word pictures.

8. *Be ambitious with team presentations.*
   You'll need to rehearse a team presentation. If you record the rehearsal, pay attention to where team members are looking when a colleague is speaking and how they're looking. Remember you're still 'on stage' even when someone else is speaking. The audience will always see bored or nervous faces or awkward posture. If everyone on stage looks at the speaker it drives the audience attention on to the speaker.

9. *Get feedback.*
   Seek continuous feedback. This gives you information to develop yourself and reveals blindspots. Consider getting a presentation buddy to regularly share and swap feedback.

Review recordings of your work and assess yourself.

10. *Be bold!*
    Believe in yourself and be bold.

That's it – you have everything you need to present like a pro. Go smash it!

Endnotes

[1] www.mayaangelou.com/blog

[2] P. Brown and V. Brown, *Neuropsychology for Coaches* (Open University Press, 2012), p.18.

[3] M. Forsyth, *The Elements of Eloquence: How to turn the perfect English phrase* (Icon Books, 2013).

[4] A. Pease and B. Pease, *The Definitive Book of Body Language* (Orion, 2005), p.189.

[5] www.ted.com/talks/brene_brown_on_vulnerability

[6] A. Pease and B. Pease, *The Definitive Book of Body Language* (Orion, 2005), p.357.

[7] B. Minto, *The Pyramid Principle: Logic in writing and thinking* (Pearson Books, 2009), p.7.

[8] A much fuller explanation of the pyramid structure is in Barbara Minto's excellent book, *The Pyramid Principle: Logic in writing and thinking* (Pearson Books, 2009).

[9] According to Allan and Barbara Pease (in *The Definitive Book of Body Language*, Orion, 2005, p.190), visual and verbal presentations have a retention rate of 50% compared to 10% for just words alone.

[10] K. Cherry, 'What Is The Serial Position Effect?', January 2017. www.explorepsychology.com/serial-position-effect/

[11] P. McAleer, A. Todorov and P. Belin, 'How do you say "hello"? Personality impressions from brief novel voices', *PLoS ONE* 9(3): e90779. doi:10.1371/ journal.pone.0090779 (2014).

[12] A. Furnham and E. Petrova, *Body Language in Business: Decoding the signals* (Palgrave Macmillan, 2010), p.57.

[13] A. Furnham and E. Petrova, *Body Language in Business: Decoding the signals* (Palgrave Macmillan, 2010), p.143.

[14] S. Stevenson, 'There's magic in your smile', *Psychology Today*, 25 June 2012.

[15] A. Furnham and E. Petrova, *Body Language in Business: Decoding the signals* (Palgrave Macmillan, 2010), p.32.

[16] R. Emmons, 'Three surprising ways that gratitude works at work', *Greater Good Magazine*, 11 October 2017.

[17] Research led by Prathik Kini, the University of Indiana, 2015.

[18] Research by P. Kini, J. Wong, S. McInnis, N. Gabana and J. W. Brown, 'The effects of gratitude expression on neural activity', *Neuroimage*, 128, 1–10 (2016).

[19] Research by P. Kini, J. Wong, S. McInnis, N. Gabana and J. W. Brown, 'The effects of gratitude expression on neural activity', *Neuroimage*, 128, 1–10 (2016).

Endnotes

[20] P. Kini, J. Wong, S. McInnis, N. Gabana and J. W. Brown, 'The effects of gratitude expression on neural activity', *Neuroimage*, 128, 1–10 (2016).

[21] R. Emmons, 'Three surprising ways that gratitude works at work', *Greater Good Magazine*, 11 October 2017.

[22] M. Normant, *Coach Yourself Up Programme Guide* (2016, p.137).

[23] Author of *Perceptual Integration: The mechanics of awakening*, Gary Sherman has 15 free recordings relating to developing attention and self-awareness, so if this topic engages you, there's plenty to explore. Mike Normant attributes much of his content on this topic to Gary Sherman.

[24] This idea was created by the late academic Chris Argyris and is widely known in the work of Peter Senge in *The Fifth Discipline: The art and practice of the learning organization* (Random House Business Books). The concept of the Ladder of Inference can also be used in reverse: you start at the top of the ladder with the action based on belief and work down the ladder to explore your thinking and assumptions. It's a useful process to explain to audiences your perspective and to make your thinking and reasoning visible. When used in this way it's often called the Ladder of Advocacy.

[25] E. Kross, *Psychology Today*, June 2015.

[26] J. Bauman, 'The gold medal mind', *Psychology Today*. Originally published in May 2000 and reviewed/updated in June 2016.

[27] This references a discussion of athletes in flow in J. Bauman, 'The gold medal mind', *Psychology Today*. Originally published in May 2000 and reviewed/updated in June 2016.

[28] Dr S. Williams, Department of Management, Raj Soin College of Business, Wright State University, Dayton, Ohio, 'Head Games: The use of mental rehearsal to improve performance', March 2004.

[29] Col V. M. Meyer, 'Sport psychology for the soldier athlete: A paradigm shift', *Military Medicine* 183(7–8), 2018. https://doi.org/10.1093/milmed/usx087

Enjoyed this?
Then you'll love…

Executive Presentations: Develop presence to speak with confidence and skill by Jacqui Harper

Short-Listed For The Business Book Awards 2019!

This book equips executives to give compelling and clear presentations: the kind of presentations that drive corporate change and innovation *and* make reputations. And it's all down to presence.

Presence works at three levels: what you say, how you use your body, and your mindset.

- Level 1: Discover how to transform ideas and business messages with a simple five-step tool.
- Level 2: Learn how to leverage your physical presence when speaking, including your style, body language and vocal presence.
- Level 3: Speak with confidence and resilience

by developing your mindset, with four powerful tools to transform the way you think as you prepare to present.

Jacqui's rich blend of tools, tips and expert advice will help you become a consistently outstanding communicator.

Jacqui Harper is called the 'presentation doctor' at INSEAD, the number one global business school (*Financial Times*, 2017), where she's a visiting professor teaching Executive Presence.

Previously a TV news anchor for the BBC, she has also presented news programmes for Sky News and ITV.

As a communication coach at Crystal Business Coaching, Jacqui has transformed Executive Presentations for over 20 years. Her clients include CEOs of global corporations and staff at the Foreign Office.

Other 6-Minute Smarts titles

Write to Think (based on *Exploratory Writing* by Alison Jones)

No-Nonsense PR (based on *Hype Yourself* by Lucy Werner)

Do Change Better (based on *How to be a Change Superhero* by Lucinda Carney)

How to be Happy at Work (based on *My Job Isn't Working!* by Michael Brown)

Mastering People Management (based on *Mission: To Manage* by Marianne Page)

Look out for more titles coming soon! Visit www.practicalinspiration.com for all our latest titles.